16x

How would you rate yourself in terms of creativity?

On a ten-point scale — with 1 being almost zero imagination, originality, or innovative ability, and 10 representing superb creative powers — where would you score? Seriously think about it. Now circle the number that you think fits:

1 2 3 4 5 6 7 8 9 10

LOW |<————————————————————————>| HIGH

This is a lot bigger deal than you might imagine. Organizations are hungry for good ideas. The smart companies know their future depends heavily on relentless improvement…on constant innovation…on break-throughs. So they're cranking up their efforts to become more creative.

This handbook positions you to help move the needle in that direction. Regardless of where you rank yourself on creativity, you can learn the mechanics of achieving breakthrough results. The 16X approach is so simple. So down to earth. But you'll see that, compared to how people and organizations typically operate, it's as unique as it is powerful.

16X is about strengths-based innovation. And it will deliver break-throughs in your personal life just as well as it does on the job.

The 16X approach works by establishing some "core conditions" that creativity and innovation flow from: white space, a focus on what counts, and the engagement of signature strengths. It's a process of finding more running room so your prime talents can flex and further develop. By getting rid of the common disabling conditions, creativity and innovation come to life, liberating your most able and talented self.

Your guide on this innovation pathway is Richard Koch. He's the most authoritative voice on Planet Earth about the breakthrough principle of 16X.

I chased down Richard via email at his home in Cape Town, South Africa, asking him to work with PRITCHETT on this handbook. He's a brilliant, fascinating, hugely successful person, and he lives his message. Beyond his best-selling books that we've quoted on the following pages, he's living proof that the concepts work.

Now, consistent with the breakthrough principle of 16X, let me end with this point. Most of what you read this week won't make a bit of difference. It will be a waste of your time. But this handbook can change your life.

—*Price Pritchett*

"Making the simple complicated is commonplace; making the complicated simple, awesomely simple, that's creativity."

—CHARLES MINGUS

PRITCHETT

The Breakthrough Principle of 16x

So how did it go for you this morning?

Most likely you climbed out of bed at about the usual time. Then you hit your routine — a familiar pattern of steps that involve getting cleaned up, clothed, and maybe caffeinated to face the day.

Heading into your closet, what did you pick to wear?

There's little doubt, out of all the articles of clothing you have to choose from, only a handful were even considered as you got dressed. The same 20 percent of your garments are what you end up wearing 80 percent of the time.

Now think of all the toiletries in the cabinets, drawers, and shelves of your bathroom. How much of that stuff do you actually use these days? It's a safe bet: The same 20 percent of those many personal items are all that you use 80 percent of the time. The rest is pretty much clutter. You hardly ever touch it.

The same peculiar pattern shows up yet again as you head to work. Out of all the possible routes you could travel, you choose the same 20 percent as the path you'll take 80 percent of the time.

And so unfolds the ordinary, everyday proof of a remarkable principle at work in your life. It's called the 80/20 principle.

This well known principle captures the lopsidedness that so often occurs between cause and effect. For example, 80 percent of results flow from 20 percent of effort…80 percent of the outputs are driven by 20 percent of inputs…80 percent of consequences are the outcome of a mere 20 percent of the causes. A fairly small amount of our time, energy, and effort is amazingly more productive than most of it. The 80/20 rule

highlights this strange but predictable imbalance between efforts and rewards.

But there's another principle that follows from the 80/20 concept, one that isn't so well known. And it holds the secret to stunning performance breakthroughs on the job as well as in your personal life.

This related principle is about practical, down-to-earth innovation. It's a creative approach any person or organization can use to escape from the routines and attitudes that trap us. It's the new story of the "16 times" principle, or 16X for short.

The *16X principle* positions you to multiply your effectiveness by a factor of 16. Let's go over that again, and make sure it sinks in. You can use the *16X principle* to become super-productive…to achieve results which are *16 times better* than what you've been getting. Maybe even more. And you can do this without experiencing a smidgen more stress or strain.

Just like the 80/20 principle that underlies it, the *16X principle* belongs to everybody. It can work for anyone and everyone. It's a realistic, ready-to-use innovation process for doing things differently, with no more effort or energy than today, to get *16 times better* results.

The amazing *16X principle* is actually easy to prove. But the important thing is to discover how powerfully it can work for you.

> "They say you can't do it, but sometimes it doesn't always work."
>
> —CASEY STENGEL

Part 1

THE BREAKTHROUGH
PROMISE OF **16x**

"The most formidable weapon for growth in business is the 80/20 principle, creatively applied by individuals and small teams of individuals. With the 80/20 principle, people can leverage the most powerful forces around them—tangible, but especially intangible ones—to dazzle the world and provide customers with much more of what they want for much less of what they wish to conserve (money, resources, time, space, and energy)."

The 80/20 Individual: How to Build
on the 20% of What You Do Best
—RICHARD KOCH

TRACING THE HISTORY
OF **16X**

The story of 16X began in Switzerland, over a hundred years ago, and it started out as a study of money.

The year was 1897. A shaggy-bearded Italian named Vilfredo Pareto — professor of economics at Lausanne University — was about to stumble onto an amazing discovery.

Pareto was curious about wealth. He wondered about the patterns of rich and poor among people all around the world. Studying many countries, across the reach of time, he was staggered to find almost exactly the same pattern showing up in every situation. Wherever he looked, a few people earned most of the money and had most of the wealth. The majority of people were poor. The imbalance was almost identical, regardless of country or time. It just always played out that way.

This unequal distribution of wealth is as predictable today as it was back then. It's like a natural law is at work, dividing people into the "haves" and "have nots."

Economists began to notice all kinds of unequal patterns, where just a few causes accounted for most of the results. They called it Pareto's Law. Only decades later was this strange phenomenon labeled "the 80/20 rule" or "the 80/20 principle." Since the 1950s, thousands of studies have shown most of any firm's profits come from a small portion of products. The large majority of sales come from a select few customers. Roughly 80 percent — sometimes only 70 percent, sometimes 90 or even 99 percent — of results come from 20 percent or less of the inputs. Indeed, Pareto had uncovered a bizarre and unbalanced relationship between cause and effect.

Here are just a few real life examples of how the 80/20 principle operates:

South Africa's leading venture capital house, Brait, recently found that 11 percent of its deals over the past 13 years had yielded 80 percent of total deal profits.

Just 12 percent of American households use personal financial management software, but they account for 75 percent of the profits made by all US banks.

5 percent of Internet sites get 75 percent of all Web traffic.

Studies in leading North American banks consistently show that 15-25 percent of each bank's customers generate 80-95 percent of the bank's profits.

In the last month, I sent 572 emails to 134 different people. My most long-suffering friend got 103 emails — 18 percent of emails to less than 1 percent of recipients. A total of 18 people received 400 emails — 70 percent of emails to just over 13 percent of people. The top 38 recipients had a total of 476 emails from me — 28 percent of correspondents got 83 percent of emails.

The 20th Century accounted for a tiny fraction of 1 percent of human history — just 0.00025 of it — but it hosted 20 percent of all human years lived since history began.

4 percent of the world's people speak 60 percent of its languages, but the most popular 1½ percent of languages are used by 90 percent of us.

The 80/20 principle is now established as *the* way that numbers work for nearly everything related to wealth, economics, business, and much of everyday life. Pareto's Law remains alive and well.

But only recently has attention begun to shift to *another* principle, one that is even more compelling than the 80/20 principle. The new discovery — the *16X principle* — is logically derived from 80/20. If the 80/20 principle is true, as countless investigations prove, then the *16X principle* is true. And that's terrific news for everyone, because it means we can all change how we do things and get 16 times greater results.

> "In the three years I played ball, we won six, lost seventeen and tied two. Some statistician...calculated that we won 75 percent of the games we didn't lose."
>
> —ROGER M. BLOUGH

"The reason that the 80/20 principle is so valuable is that it is counterintuitive. We tend to expect that all causes will have roughly the same significance...that 50 percent of causes or inputs will account for 50 percent of results or outputs... But this '50/50 fallacy' is one of the most inaccurate and harmful, as well as the most deeply rooted, of our mental maps...We may feel that some of our time is more valuable than the rest, but if we measure inputs and outputs the disparity can still stun us."

The 80/20 Principle: The Secret
of Achieving More with Less
—RICHARD KOCH

THE AMAZING MATH
OF **80/20**

It's been proven time and time again that roughly 80 percent of results arise from only 20 percent of energy. That's mind-boggling enough. But this means that the best bits of our time, energy, or effort produce *16 times better results* than most of our energy.

Puzzled? I'm not surprised. The first time I worked this out, I was dumb-founded. I thought I must have it wrong. But no, it's true. And here's why.

Imagine that you're a salesperson and, to keep the math simple, you have just ten customers. You're paid on a commission basis, so you get a certain amount (for these purposes it doesn't matter how much) for every dollar of sales you make. Each customer requires the same effort from you. They call you up, you take the order, you arrange delivery and fill in your sales report.

Two of your customers are big. Every day they each buy $400 worth of what you sell. The other eight customers are small, and every day they each buy $25 worth of goods.

If you add up the sales of the two big customers, they total $800 a day. The eight small customers spend $25 each, for a daily total of $200. That adds up to $1,000 a day sold by you. This fits the 80/20 principle. Two out of ten customers — 20 percent — buy 80 percent of what you sell ($800 out of $1,000 is 80%). So far, no surprises. But let's look at your effort and your rewards from the big customers, then compare that to what happens with the small customers.

The big customers give you 80 percent of your sales and commission. But because there are only two of them, out of 10 customers in total, they only take 20 percent of your energy. So your return on investment is 80 units of reward for 20 units of effort. If we divide 80 by 20, we see that you get a "payback factor" of 4.

Now for the small customers. Remember, they give you 20 percent of your overall sales and commission. Because there are eight of them, out of ten customers in total, they take 80 percent of your energy. Your return on investment here is 20 units of reward for 80 units of effort. The "payback factor" here is 20 divided by 80 — 0.25 — or only a quarter of one.

Now, consider how the "payback factor" of 4 for the big customers stacks up against the 0.25 you're getting from your small customers. The math is simple, but the message is amazing: The "payback factor" of 4 is *16 times* greater than the 0.25! In other words, from your point of view, the big customers are 16 times better than the small customers. The energy you put into the big guys will give you 16 times what you get from the same amount of energy devoted to the small fry.

This sounds crazy, but it's true. And while it's easy to see that big customers are much better than small customers (provided they pay the same prices and take the same amount of effort), that's not the main point. The main point is that, as a rule, the best 20 percent of your energy produces results that are 16 times better than what's produced by your other 80 percent.

If you think about this, you'll discover three breakthrough insights for how to run your life or organization:

⊙ Knowing the best uses of your energy is much more important than trying harder or working longer. To get 16 times better results, you don't have to do anything essentially different from what you're already doing at the moment. You just have to do more of what you're already doing that works fantastically well.

⊙ Most of what you do is a waste of time. Compared to the few things that work fantastically well, it's dust in the scales. You might as well *stop* most of what you do!

⊙ You can put less energy in, yet get far better results, if you just concentrate on the things that produce fantastic results.

Of course, the math in 16X only applies if the relationship between energy and results is exactly 80/20. So it's best to think of the 80/20 formula as only a rule of thumb. If the true ratio is 75/25, then you'll "only" get 9 times better results from the top things you do. Sometimes the true ratio turns out to be 90/10, though, which gives you a massive 81 times better results.

Regardless, here's the point. If you learn to use the *16X principle*, you won't be doing things a little bit better or even twice as well. You'll make things 5, 10, 15, 20 or even 100 times better, compared to most of your effort today.

> "It's not an optical illusion. It just looks like one."
>
> —STEVEN WRIGHT

"Creation is not a mysterious process, confined to the scientific genius, the mad inventor, or the entrepreneur. Creation can be engineered, if you understand what drives it. Individuals and ideas drive creation. It happens in predictable and repeatable ways. If we understand this, we can create."

The 80/20 Individual: How to Build
on the 20% of What You Do Best
—RICHARD KOCH

CREATING WHITE SPACE
FOR
Innovation

The *16X principle* tells us that large performance breakthroughs are always possible. But most people don't pull them off. What accounts for this?

Well, some people can't get past their skepticism. They think the promise of 16X sounds too good to be true. The idea of doing less, yet accomplishing far more, just doesn't seem feasible to them.

Also, most people are mentally locked in to the idea of gradual improvement. At the risk of oversimplifying things, let's say there are always two types of approach — the popular one that may be pretty good, mediocre, or weak, plus a rare one that works extremely well. Ordinarily, people focus on the popular approach, tweaking it as their way of seeking improvements. The trap they fall into is trying to make things just a little bit better. They put their faith in working harder. Or working longer. And they miss out on 16X because they only think in terms of marginal improvements. That's just the usual way.

But since 16X is a proven, scientific principle — like the 80/20 rule from which it comes — we can be confident that huge improvement truly is available. It just calls for a new way of looking at things. Breakthroughs come from a fresh approach allied with powerful principles. They come from *innovation*…from doing *new* things, or from doing old things in a *new way*. If we can find the approach that's uniquely powerful, we can get a large multiplication of results.

So instead of throwing more effort at whatever situation or problem you face, consider which efforts you could discontinue. The mechanics of 16X are more about stopping than starting to do more. The key is to create white space — in your schedule…in your mind…in your life as a whole. It's about emptying your days of those things that don't justify your time and effort because they give such a poor return.

Many of the things you allow to take up space in your life are not important. They accumulated gradually over a period of years — certain work habits, leisure activities, relationships, stuff lying around your home, and a lot more that you could add to the list. But so much of what's there has lost most of whatever importance or utility it ever had in the first place.

Just think — what would it be like if you scaled back to those things that truly count the most? That work the very best? That bring you the greatest joy, energy, and sense of fulfillment? How much more time, vitality, and peace would that bring? Then imagine taking some of this new white space you've created by uncluttering your life, and investing it in those things that count most, work best, and bring the greatest rewards. That's your path to breakthrough results.

Once again, 16X improvement is always attainable. But it stands to reason that such a large leap of progress won't come without a little thought and experimentation. It won't come from following the herd. It won't come, however hard we try, from doing again today what we did yesterday. It will only come from a reallocation of our personal resources— for example our time, energy, and talents. We must be innovative in handling our jobs and lives, doing things differently on a day-to-day basis.

Don't get the idea that 16X is a complex process. And don't presume that while it might work for some people, it really can't for you. The *16X principle* works all the time in the world — for someone, somewhere, every second of the day. And you can put it to work for you.

> "There is no pleasure in having nothing to do; the fun is having lots to do and not doing it."
>
> —JOHN W. RAPER

Part **2**

THE FIVE PRACTICES
OF 16x

"The way to create something great is to create something simple...progress requires simplicity; and simplicity requires ruthlessness. This helps to explain why simple is as rare as it is beautiful."

The 80/20 Principle: The Secret of Achieving More with Less
—RICHARD KOCH

FOCUS.

FOCUS

FOCUS.

Once upon a time there was a failed British politician. His father had been laughed out of politics. He himself had been influential in taking Britain into the First World War, a horrific disaster. During that war, he sent a large force to Gallipoli in Turkey. The troops were massacred as soon as they arrived. He went on to become the worst Finance Minister in living memory. He changed parties twice, ending up distrusted and disliked by most of his colleagues. On top of all this, he was an alcoholic, and prone to spells of deep depression.

Yet he was *focused*. He wanted to become Prime Minister of Britain. That was all he cared about, all he dreamed about, all he worked toward. And he was focused in another way. Throughout the 1930s, he identified one issue that he thought was very important, and he kept banging on about it. He thought that Germany was a lethal threat to the British Empire. He was scorned as a bore, as well as a drunk.

The man was Winston Churchill. On June 10, 1940, to general surprise, he was made Prime Minister. "I felt as if I were walking with destiny," he wrote that night, "and that all of my past life had been but a preparation for this hour." He was focused. That was the only reason he won the job.

Those were dark days. Churchill knew the only way Britain could beat Hitler was to get the United States into the war. Now he focused on that. And he won again.

Focus is magical. And the magic comes from the *16X principle*.

What gives great results? Always, a very few things. So the secret is in finding the few things that are really powerful — truly pivotal — which make the difference between success and failure.

Care about those things. Care about nothing else. Do those things. Do nothing else. To the extent that you possibly can, focus your work and your life on those areas where the "payback factor" is huge.

Actually, this principle holds true regardless of the task or challenge at hand. So the first step is to figure out the few vital things. In any task, most of the things that are done hardly matter. But a few things matter a great deal. Sometimes it's just one thing that counts, like getting America into Churchill's war.

So, let's say that you're given a project at work — to win an important new customer…hire a new staff person…create an advertising campaign… organize a set of data…or whatever. There are a million and one ways you could try to do this. But most likely, very few of them stand much chance of producing extraordinary results. So focus on the one or two things with the most promise.

Step two is to cut out everything else. We always seem to be short of resources, whether it's money, time, people, contacts, or energy. But the truth is, we're not really short of these things at all. Most of the time we squander our resources and opportunities. And that happens because we're not focused.

If we bore in on a few objectives, or better still on just one, we find we have loads of resources with which to pursue the goal. To do this, though, we need to stop wasting effort on things that don't matter.

Why not give it a shot? Next time you have an important assignment or objective, work out the way to crack it, and then stop doing anything else. By abandoning the low payoff efforts and unrelated activities, you free up precious time you can use to do much more of the few things that truly matter. For Churchill, it was getting close to President Roosevelt. What is it for you? Whatever it is, do more of it, and do it better. Once again, you'll have plenty of time, and lots of support. Because you'll be doing so much less of everything else.

Quitting is a key aspect of learning to innovate via the 16X formula. Let go of the trivial many. Focus on the vital few.

"If quitters never win, and winners never quit, then who is the fool who said 'Quit while you're ahead.'?"

—UNKNOWN

"You can identify the mass of irrelevant and low-value activity and begin to shed this worthless skin. You can isolate the parts of your character, work style, lifestyle, and relationships that, measured against the time or energy involved, give you value many times greater than the daily grind; and, having isolated them, you can, with no little courage and determination, multiply them. You can become a better, more useful and happier human being. And you can help others to do the same."

The 80/20 Principle: The Secret
of Achieving More with Less
—RICHARD KOCH

DEFY THE TYRANNY
OF **Routine.**

We're all creatures of habit. Sure, we like the idea of making big improvements, but none of us *really* likes change. So we plow on, mindlessly doing the same old things in the same old way. It comes natural. Trouble is, our routines close our minds and lives to the breakthroughs that we say we want.

Of course, some of our habits are valuable. Familiar routines can be efficient and economical, freeing us from having to think. So if we get into the habit, for example, of daily exercise, visiting an elderly neighbour, or reading a worthy book that makes us think, we can do ourselves enormous good without having to gear up for it. We don't waste any time or energy trying to figure out what to do, yet we replenish the wellsprings of our bodies, hearts, and minds.

Sadly, too many of our habits are not of this ilk. Even if the habits themselves apparently do no harm, they confine us in lives that are smaller than they could be.

Habit and routine are the enemies of innovation. They put boundaries around our performance. Like gravity, they keep us on the ground, stifling our imagination and preventing our lives from soaring to new heights.

Our habits are ordinarily quiet. Inconspicuous. But they're tyrants at heart — insidious bullies — that trap us in our everyday routines. And no tyrant in the whole of history has ever been overcome without defiance. No tyrant has been ousted without a fight. No tyrant has departed due to business as usual.

So if we want to innovate, if we want to capture the 16X promise, we have to defy some of our routines. We have to make a conscious effort to think about things differently. Note that I start by saying, "think about things differently," not "do things differently." We cannot do things in new, meaningful, more productive ways unless we've first thought about things from fresh angles.

Thinking — real thinking, new thinking, innovative thinking — is hard. That's why we rush around "doing things." If we're really busy, we leave ourselves no time to merely think. And make no mistake, thinking can cause us discomfort. Thinking is lonely. Thinking makes us vulnerable — it challenges our sacred cows…exposes us to possible embarrassment and ridicule…subverts our ego and our emotions. Also, when we think about innovation and change, we're in danger of interfering with the preferences or habit patterns of our friends, bosses, colleagues, and loved ones. Even worse, we're in danger of contradicting ourselves, or concluding that we're on wrong path — maybe just going helter-skelter in no particular direction — in our work or our lives.

But if new thinking is hard and wrenching, it's also the road to freedom and to fulfilling our destiny as human beings. Other animals are totally the prisoners of instinct, of routine, of their genes. For example, a rabbit never stops to ask why she is excavating a burrow. No cat ever queries whether it should chase a mouse. Likewise, we humans are heavily subject to instinct, our genes, and the tyranny of routine. But we can break free.

The *16X principle* excites us with the reality that genuine, solid, and massive improvement is possible. But to grasp that reality, to make that progress, we have to innovate. To innovate, we have to defy routine. We have to think — anew, ambitiously, and preferably with outrageous demands.

Happily, overcoming the tyranny of routine can itself become commonplace. The first time you defy routine it nearly kills you. The second time, it's really tough. The third time, it's merely hard. Some way down the road, it becomes, if not easy, then reasonably comfortable. Your confidence grows, and the tyrant loses a large part of its hold on you.

So start challenging your routines. The next time you run into a brick wall, stop beating your head against it. Pause. Think. Find a new way that goes around the wall, or maybe over it. Look for a new approach that is 10, 16, 20, or 100 times better. Rest assured, the new way is there. It does exist.

The thing is, you'll never find 16X without stopping…without thinking… without imagination. Because the breakthrough depends on you doing something creative and different.

"If you try to fail and succeed, which have you done?"

—GEORGE CARLIN

"High performers are not 10 or 20 times more intelligent than other people, it is the methods and resources they use that are unusually powerful."

Living the 80/20 Way: Work Less, Worry Less, Succeed More, Enjoy More
—RICHARD KOCH

DO IT
YOUR WAY.

Twice a week I play tennis at a local club. They have a "mix-in" where we play doubles with different partners and opponents. But since pretty much the same folks turn up most times, you get to know everyone's game. I used to be puzzled why, with the same partner and the same opponents, sometimes we won 6-0 or 6-1 and sometimes they won just as easily. Then I noticed it wasn't random. The pattern was that my partner and I won when we managed to play our type of game, with lots of high lobs to slow the game down and make the other side run. We lost when our rivals dictated their game, a rapid fire of serve and volleys, where force and accuracy counted more than fitness and endurance.

Not just in sports, but in every part of our lives, we are all profoundly different. And in spite of the myth of the "all-rounder," there are usually just a small number of things at which we excel as individuals. The difference between successful and unsuccessful people is not that the former are necessarily so much better at what they do. It's that they devote themselves so much better to doing what they do best.

And anyone can do that. So anyone can be successful, though most people aren't. The reason? Most folks limit their achievement level by doing the wrong things. Instead of playing to their greatest strengths — doing the few things they're brilliant at — you'll see them struggling to play somebody else's game.

That's why it's so important to do things "your way." Nobody else could be Frank Sinatra. But we can all "do it our way."

The easiest and most enjoyable way to excel at work, plus have a happier life of high achievement, is to invest more in your best talents. That starts with you figuring out where you shine the most. You have to identify your strong suits before you can play to them on a consistent basis. So ask yourself what you're brilliant at, then ask two or three of the friends you trust and who have good insight into your personality.

Next, think back to the last time you were "in the zone" — that is, you were totally absorbed in what you were doing, performing naturally, easily, and impressively. It might have been at work or pursuing a hobby, in a social setting or off by yourself. But you hit that state called "flow," where everything just clicked and felt like the authentic "you." This is another clue to your best 20 percent (or less) that produces 80 percent (or more) of your impact and happiness.

I call these few distinctive strengths your "20 percent spike." You should exercise your spike on a daily basis. Cultivate it…become obsessed with it. This is the most powerful you. It's where your passion lives, where your very best potential can be found. Instead of worrying about strengthening your other 80 percent, file the edge of your 20 percent spike. Being sharply pointed can make you far more effective and happier than being well-rounded.

We typically use our areas of brilliance only a small amount of the time and in a small part of our working life. This prevents us from experiencing the power of 16X. The best and most enjoyable way to transform our work and the rest of our lives is to go from using our best talents in a small part of our life to using them intensely across the full spectrum.

This takes some serious thought. You'll need to change some habits. But your happiness and your value to other people depend on it.

Now you don't have to do it all at once. Try small steps first. See if they work. Then begin to take bigger, bolder steps. Keep going until your behavior and approach are centered almost completely around the engagement of your strongest suits. Any time you're faced with a difficult challenge, stop to ask yourself one simple question: "How would I tackle this task if I made myself use only my signature strengths?" The answer will likely surprise yourself and other observers. It probably will suggest a totally new way of dealing with the issue at hand.

Granted, sometimes we have limited freedom to do things "our way." Practically every day we all face responsibilities that simply don't call our strengths into play. That's life. But if you work at it, you can progressively carve out more space to do things that exploit your 20 percent spike.

Demonstrate to your boss that if you're given more headroom, you can use your spike to get 16X results on that part of your work. If your boss listens and you deliver, you'll get more and more space. Organizations are stubborn things, but they generally respect results.

> "Always remember that you're unique. Just like everyone else."
>
> —UNKNOWN

"Exceptional individual performance requires allies...
nothing is more important than your choice of
alliances and how you build them. Without them
you are nothing. With them, you can transform
your life, often the lives of those around you, and
occasionally, in small or large ways, the course
of history."

The 80/20 Principle: The Secret
of Achieving More with Less
—RICHARD KOCH

RECRUIT THE SUPPORT OF POTENT **Allies.**

We've seen how vital it is to play our own game...to innovate "our way"...to emphasize our areas of brilliance in pursuit of 16X. But ego and vanity need to be kept on a tight leash. Once you have some leeway to do things your way, the next great leap forward is to find a few influential individuals who can leverage your efforts 16 times.

I owe my professional and financial success almost entirely to four other people. I've written elsewhere about two of them, my partners in our consulting firm LEK. Now for the first time I'd like to explain the role played by two other people. My intent is to explain how important others can be in our work lives, plus show how it's always possible to find and enlist the people who can make *your* career take off.

My first real break came when two partners and I started our own consulting firm in 1983. We knew how to do really useful work for clients. But we had no clients and no network. So we teamed up with a big, established, rather old-fashioned British-based consultancy called PA that had lots of clients. The arrangement worked okay, but there were two issues. First, they took half our profits. Second, only two people at PA opened their clients to us on any scale.

One of these was Peter Lawson, a senior PA board member with a fantastic network of contacts he had never let down. Peter could leverage our business enormously, if we could get him to join us and use his network for LEK. That way we could end our deal with PA, keep all of our profits, and yet sell even more business than before.

How could we persuade Peter? Chemistry would take us part of the way. I really liked Peter, and thought he would like me if I spent time getting to know him. So I did. But to get him to sign up with LEK, I had to know his "hot buttons" that really turned him on. What excited Peter was building links between business, government, and politics. So Peter and I worked out a deal where he became chairman of an LEK "advisory board" made up of leading industrialists and politicians. As a result, LEK gained an enormous amount of business.

In 1989 I sold my stake in LEK to my partners, and had some money to invest. My idea was to find firms that had fallen on hard times but which had a leading market position and could be rebuilt. I could identify the firms and devise a new strategy for them. But I needed someone who could do the hard work of turning the firms around in practice. Step forward Robin Field, a fellow I had recruited into LEK who had become a friend. The first turnaround we identified was Filofax, a wonderful brand and business that, through bad management and strategy, was going bust. We bought a stake in the business. Robin became CEO and duly turned it round, multiplying investors' money seven times. After that triumph, I had the credibility and deal flow to find lots of other great investments. Since then I have multiplied my money many, many times.

How did I persuade Robin to join me? As with Peter, it was partly because we got on well, and partly because I identified and hit his hot buttons. I knew that Robin hated being a consultant, even though he was well paid. He wanted to get back to running businesses. But he also liked the

"deal" aspect of having a stake in the business. So I was able to offer Robin exactly what he wanted.

Here's the point. You shouldn't think of 16X as strictly a solo act. Even if you're blessed with magnificent personal talents and drive, other people with different strengths and ambitions can greatly enhance your success. They can make it happen faster, easier, and better. All of us can achieve tens or hundreds times more if we team up with the right people.

The key to 16X collaboration is making careful choices. We need only *very few* people to help us. If you made a list of a hundred people who potentially could help, nearly all of the actual benefit to you probably would come from a handful of them. Certainly fewer than 20 people, more likely somewhere between 1 person and 5, would bring 80 percent or more of the value.

So start out targeting the top people, the handful who can *help you most.* You may think you're shooting too high. Shoot anyway. Once you've identified these individuals, get to know them and figure out their "hot buttons." They're not likely to help you unless the chemistry is excellent and the relationship brings obvious value to them. Get them excited, and you're more than half way there.

> "If it's true that we are here to help others, then what exactly are the others here for?"
> —GEORGE CARLIN

"80 percent of value is created by concentrating on 20 percent of issues within a market, by innovating accordingly. 80 percent of value comes from 20 percent of changes. What demands are changing? Who is driving progress? How? Could you copy it, do it cheaper, take it to a new place, or take it further?"

Living the 80/20 Way: Work Less, Worry Less, Succeed More, Enjoy More
—RICHARD KOCH

RECYCLE THE WORLD'S
BEST IDEAS.

The fifth and final route to 16X performance is to leverage the few great ideas that already stalk the earth. Powerful ideas are out there, available free, just waiting to be applied to a new context.

Andrew Black is the greatest innovator and genius that I know personally. He invented the idea of person-to-person betting, cutting out the book-maker. He was ideally suited to do this, as a brilliant mathematician, former professional gambler, and technology enthusiast. As a result, he's made a fortune, and the company he founded — Betfair — will soon be worth billions of dollars. I know all about this because I invested in his company soon after it started.

But Andrew's idea of a person-to-person betting exchange is less revolu-tionary than it appears. In fact, it's just the idea of a stock exchange, recycled from the investment industry to the gaming industry. Instead of one person selling stock and another buying it, one person makes a bet and another person makes an opposite bet.

Amidst the greatest triumphs of technology and business the universe has ever known, there really is nothing new under the sun. This is great news for you and me. We can take proven ideas and tweak them to drive our own innovations.

The truth is, out of the tens of thousands of business ideas ever tried, there's a tiny percentage, and a tiny number, that deliver the great majority of value. I believe we can boil it down to these ten top priority ideas.

The 10 Great Business Ideas of All Time

1. **Market Leadership.** *Be the biggest of your type.*

2. **Low Cost Volume.** *Be the cheapest.*

3. **Build on Your Strengths.** *Make your best attributes even stronger.*

4. **Delegate.** *Train a lower cost person.*

5. **Self-Service.** *Make the customer do the heavy lifting.*

6. **Subtract Something.** *Differentiate by deleting.*

7. **Create a New Niche Category.** *Split an existing category into two.*

8. **Personalize.** *Let customers tailor your offering.*

9. **Do It Faster.** *Use speed to justify a higher price tag while lowering production costs.*

10. **Do It Smaller.** *Go "little" to reduce costs and increase convenience.*

Each one of these ideas might provide 16X, 160X, or 1,600X leverage to any new project you undertake. So run down this list systematically and ask whether each one might be applied to your situation. Experiment. Try variants and let the market pick the winner. Look for unexpected successes. If you see proof of market approval, ride the tiger!

If none of these angles delivers for you, that's very unusual. Try *combining* two of the great ideas and adapting them to your product or market. Sooner or later, you'll hit on a big winner.

Remember, you don't have to be completely original. Taking an idea that's worked elsewhere is the expeditious pathway to a 16X solution. "Elsewhere" can mean in a different country, town, or type of customer market. It might mean a different product, service, technology or distribution channel. If the idea has worked somewhere else, you have a ready-made template for innovation. Just adapt the idea to your circumstances and test it. Once you realize that pure originality is unnecessary, innovation becomes possible any place at any time.

> "Originality usually amounts only to plagiarizing something unfamiliar."
> —KATHERINE FULLERTON GEROULD

"The power of the 80/20 principle lies in the fact that it is not fully intuitive. Although we do expect some things to be more important than others, we don't expect the differences between the important things and the less important things to be anywhere near as great as they usually are...'Less is more' is a useful catch phrase because it reminds us that much of what we do, when closely analyzed, has negative value. Many activities, customers, products and suppliers actually *subtract* value, which helps to explain why their very positive counterparts produce such a high proportion of net value."

The Natural Laws of Business: How to Harness
the Power of Evolution, Physics, and Economics
to Achieve Business Success
—RICHARD KOCH

Endnote

Let's begin with a quick review of the fundamentals. The breakthrough principle of 16X states that there are always a few approaches which are at least 16 times more fertile than the conventional ways of working.

And once again, here are the five practices of 16X:

Focus. Focus. Focus.

Most people do too much. Their lives are cluttered with unnecessary stuff and a confusing, burdensome array of choices. They waste themselves responding to the urgent while ignoring the important. They're busy, yet they're not all that effective. And they try too hard. In contrast, 16X innovators are focused and calm. They concentrate on the most important issue, and on the one best way to deal with it.

Defy the tyranny of routine.

Most people are slaves to their habits...prisoners of routines, assumptions, and a small view of the world. But 16X innovators defy routine, question their own assumptions, and give themselves time to think hard about how 80/20 applies to their lives.

Do it your way.

Most people are conformists. They're afraid to stand out, afraid to be themselves. Meanwhile, 16X innovators do it "their way," relentlessly seeking ever greater opportunities to deploy their signature strengths. They're centered; the world revolves around what they value and believe is important.

Recruit the support of potent allies.

Most people rely too much on themselves, foregoing great advantages they could readily have by enlisting the support of others. Some give up their ambitions and big ideas without ever trying, presuming they would have to do it all by themselves. Others press on in their solitary efforts. But 16X innovators know that to pursue big dreams and exploit major breakthroughs, self is never enough. They target a few great allies, cultivate those relationships, and collaborate for mutual gain.

Recycle the world's best ideas.

Most people believe that new ideas have to be totally original. Since pure originality is extraordinarily difficult, they give up on innovation. But 16X innovators use great ideas from the past and present to fuel their innovations.

Okay. With those five practices fresh in your mind, now sit back and think. Give yourself time to figure out several things.

For example, what do you want or need to do? *Really.* Try to step outside your routine ways of thinking and seeing the world. Take a fresh look. Be sure you're aiming at the right target.

Hold these three questions in front of yourself:

- *What things truly count the most?*
- *What works the very best?*
- *What brings me the greatest joy, energy, and sense of fulfillment?*

Let those thoughts give shape to your intentions. Let your answers guide your approach.

Then, by way of starting to implement the *16X principle*, consider what to stop doing…what to get rid of…what to ignore. Identify specific things you can empty from your life. Before you begin to do *more* of anything, start doing *less* of something. Create white space in your everyday world.

Next, consider what you should do differently. And if you can find something that's working fantastically well, use the new white space to do more of it.

The rules of 16X are actually very simple. Relentlessly follow the five practices, and you'll position yourself to achieve 16 times better results.

> "I'm trying to arrange my life so I don't even have to be present."
>
> —UNKNOWN

"What isn't tried won't work."

—CLAUDE McDONALD

Books by PRITCHETT, LP

- *After the Merger: The Authoritative Guide for Integration Success**
- *Business As UnUsual: The Handbook for Managing and Supervising Organizational Change**
- *Carpe Mañana: 10 Critical Leadership Practices for Managing Toward the Future*
- *Culture Shift: The Employee Handbook for Changing Corporate Culture**
- *The Employee Guide to Mergers and Acquisitions**
- *The Employee Handbook for Organizational Change**
- *The Employee Handbook for Shaping Corporate Culture: The Mission Critical Approach to Culture Integration and Culture Change**
- *The Employee Handbook of New Work Habits for a Radically Changing World: 13 Ground Rules for Job Success**
- *The Employee Handbook of New Work Habits for The Next Millennium: 10 Ground Rules for Job Success*
- *The Ethics of Excellence*
- *Fast Growth: A Career Acceleration Strategy*
- *Firing Up Commitment During Organizational Change**
- *Hard Optimism: Developing Deep Strengths for Managing Uncertainty, Opportunity, Adversity, and Change**
- *High-Velocity Culture Change: A Handbook for Managers**
- *The Leadership Engine: Building Leaders at Every Level**
- *Making Mergers Work: A Guide to Managing Mergers and Acquisitions**
- *Managing Sideways: A Process-Driven Approach for Building the Corporate Energy Level and Becoming an "Alpha Company"**
- *The Mars Pathfinder Approach to "Faster-Better-Cheaper": Hard Proof From the NASA/JPL Pathfinder Team on How Limitations Can Guide You to Breakthroughs*
- *Mergers: Growth in the Fast Lane**
- *MindShift: The Employee Handbook for Understanding the Changing World of Work*
- *Outsourced: 12 New Rules for Running Your Career in an Interconnected World*
- *The Quantum Leap Strategy*
- *Resistance: Moving Beyond the Barriers to Change*
- *Service Excellence!**
- *Smart Moves: A Crash Course on Merger Integration Management**
- *A Survival Guide to the Stress of Organizational Change**
- *Team ReConstruction: Building a High Performance Work Group During Change**
- *Teamwork: The Team Member Handbook**
- *Topgrading: How to Hire, Coach and Keep A Players**
- *you^2: A High-Velocity Formula for Multiplying Your Personal Effectiveness in Quantum Leaps*

---

*Training program also available. Please call 1-800-992-5922 for more information on our training or international rights and foreign translations.

RICHARD KOCH is the author of 14 acclaimed books, including the best-selling *80/20* trilogy — *The 80/20 Principle* (over 700,000 copies sold), *The 80/20 Individual*, and *Living the 80/20 Way*. As well as lecturing and broadcasting, he is an extremely successful entrepreneur and investor. His ventures have included Filofax, Plymouth Gin, and currently Betfair, the world's largest betting exchange. Formerly he was a consultant with the Boston Consulting Group, a partner of Bain & Company, and a founder of LEK Consulting. He now has homes in London, Cape Town, and the south of Spain.

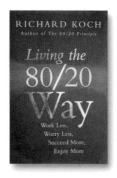

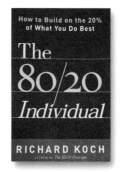

16x

YOUR ORGANIZATION.

Call 800-992-5922

or visit us at www.pritchettnet.com

for information on PRITCHETT's

application tools and services for

strengths-based innovation.

1-49 copies	____ copies at $6.95 each
50-99 copies	____ copies at $6.50 each
100-999 copies	____ copies at $5.95 each
1,000-4,999 copies	____ copies at $5.75 each
5,000-9,999 copies	____ copies at $5.50 each
10,000 or more copies	____ copies at $5.25 each

Please reference
special customer number 10516X
when ordering.

Name _____

Job Title _____

Organization _____

Address _____

City, State _____ Zip Code _____

Country _____ Phone _____ Fax _____

Email _____

Purchase order number (if applicable) _____

*Applicable sales tax, shipping and handling charges
will be added. Prices subject to change.
Orders less than $250 require prepayment.
Orders of $250 or more may be invoiced.*

☐ Check Enclosed   ☐ Please Invoice

☐ **VISA**   ☐ **MasterCard**   ☐ **AMERICAN EXPRESS**

Name on Card _____

Card Number _____ Expiration Date _____

Signature _____ Date _____

TO ORDER
By phone: 800-992-5922
Online: www.pritchettnet.com
Call for our mailing address or fax number.

PRITCHETT
Dallas, Texas